CATS'
LETTERS
TO SANTA

CATS'
LETTERS
TO SANTA

compiled and edited by
BILL ADLER

illustrations by
PAUL BACON

Carroll & Graf Publishers, Inc.
New York

CATS' LETTERS TO SANTA

Carroll & Graf Publishers
An Imprint of Avalon Publishing Group, Inc.
245 West 17th Street
11th Floor
New York, NY 10011

AVALON

Text copyright © 1995, 2006 by Bill Adler
Illustration copyright © 1995 by Paul Bacon

First Carroll & Graf edition 1995
Second Carroll & Graf edition 2006

Library of Congress Cataloging-in-Publication Data is available.

ISBN-10: 0-7867-1801-3
ISBN-13: 978-0-78671-801-6

9 8 7 6 5 4 3 2

Printed in the United States of America
Distributed by Publishers Group West

*Dedicated to Barney and all the
Other Wonderful Kittens and Cats
Who Still Believe in Santa Claus*

CATS'
LETTERS
TO SANTA

Dear Santa:

Have you considered using cats instead of reindeer? Here are the reasons why:

1. **Cats eat less.**
2. **We make faster deliveries of presents because most houses have dogs and we move very swiftly when dogs are around.**
3. **We're softer.**
4. **We make nicer sounds.**
5. **Children are more likely to leave out snacks for you if they know that you're traveling with cats.**

Rudolph

Dear Santa:

I like your whiskers—they look like mine.

Perry

Dear Santa:

I could really use a few more lives. I lost one the other day on the balcony railing. A few months back I misplaced one in a tight spot behind the refrigerator. If you could just replace these two, I promise to be more careful with them.

Mehitabel

Dear Santa:

I live in New York City. There are no chimneys here. You'll have to be buzzed in by the doorman.

Affectionally,

Madison

Dear Santa:

If I'm napping when you stop by, please wake me. I want to say hello and thank you for the wonderful mouse you got for me last year. (That was from you, right?) I had a great time chasing it around the house, and when I captured the mouse, I dropped it in my masters' bed. Boy were they happy—you should have seen them scream for joy.

P.S. I usually sleep under the couch in the living room.

Butch

Dear Santa:

Can you make that ray of sunshine stay put, even on cloudy days?

Smiley

Dear Santa:

Please don't come down the chimney.

    It's very dirty

    I know.

    I tried.

                  Your friend,

                  Jiminey

Dear Santa:

I'm not asking for anything for myself, but I think that little fish in the tank is very lonely since his companion mysteriously disappeared. Could you send a dozen or so playmates? The really colorful ones with the long wavy fins that stick up out of the top of the tank are the easiest to scoop up with a paw—um, I mean they're the kind that other fish likes for company.

Selflessly yours,

Snowball

Dear Santa Claus:

Please leave me a new set of claws.

They declawed me.

Rudy

Dear Santa:

I'd like some new curtains for the windows.
The old ones we had were pretty good for
climbing though I have to say, it was getting
tougher and tougher for me to find good
claw-gripping spots—but now we don't have
them anymore. For some reason, the people
took them down, making all kinds of
muttering noises, and they haven't put
anything back up! Please, Santa, bring them
soon, because I really *need* to see what's on
top of the bookcase these days.

Thanks,

Freddie

Dear Santa:

Please find me a new family.

I'm allergic to this bunch.

Patty

Dear Santa:

I desperately need an electric razor.

My whiskers are too long.

                                        Steve

Dear Santa:

Could you do anything to arrange more naptimes during the day? I just don't seem to be getting enough sleep. Lately, I've only managed seven or eight naps during the day, when I used to get ten or eleven at least.

> **Love,**
>
> **Sleepy**

Dear Santa:

Can I have a bird feeder all my own? You can leave it in the window, the one that cranks open but has no screen.

> **Thanks**
>
> **Fuzzy**

Dear Santa:

**Remember my request from last Christmas
to enjoy a little more moonlight romance?
Well, I just don't seem to want that anymore—I'm not sure why. I *think* it all started
about when I came back from that awful
overnight stay at the animal hospital. Lately,
all I seem to want to do is lie around the
house and eat. So this year, forget the
amorous adventures and just fill my stocking
with some yummies for my tummy.**

Blanche

Dear Santa:

Would you like a cat for Xmas?

I am going to have kittens next week.

Pam

Dear Santa Claus:

I want a dead mouse so they will think I'm doing my job and get off my back.

Thank you,

Herman

Dear Santa:

I'd like a nice twelve-year aged-in-an-old-sock hand-selected, single-stalk catnip. Smooth, with a nice nose, and just a little bit of a bite to it.

Jean-Claude

Dear Santa:

Is it really fun being Santa Claus? Wouldn't you rather be a cat and just lay around all day? It's a lot more fun to play with wrapping paper than to wrap with wrapping paper.

Garfield

Dear Santa:

I'm sorry that I didn't leave anything for you last year. I was busy chasing mice. That's my job, just like you job is bringing good cats (such as myself) wonderful toys. Thanks in advance.

                                    Killer

Dear Santa:

I've been good this year! In case nobody told you, I didn't eat their parakeet, even though he looked delicious.

                                    Love,

                                    Sylvester

Dear Santa:

My owners always enter me in the cat show and I never win.

Could you give me a present (perhaps a membership to some kind of weight loss program?) that would help me win so they won't bother me anymore?

Thank you

Suki

Dear Santa Claus:

Do you know the Lion King?

I would like to meet him. I think we come from the same family.

Love,

Max

Dear Santa:

Here's what I've been doing each day, all year long. I wake up, I eat, I take a little nap, then I jump around a little, then I take a little nap, eat, go exploring, nap again, scratch for a while in some places that need scratching, groom myself, nap, tangle and untangle some things, eat, nap, groom myself again, and nap. Haven't I been a very good kitty?

Ed

Dear Santa:

Do you have an exercise video for cats?

Everybody says I'm a fat cat.

Your friend,

Sheldon

Dear Santa:

I'd like a couple of new houseplants this Christmas. I particularly like those spider plants, with those enticing little parts that dangle down. And could you send the plants in macramé hangers? As for the length, they should hang just high enough to be a challenge but not so high that I have no chance to make them come crashing down.

Tarzan

Dear Santa:

I would like to star in a Disney movie.

I am very cute but I need an agent.

Thank you,

Lauren

Dear Santa:

There are six cats in this house.

Could you take five and give them to some kids who asked you for a cat for Xmas?

> Thank you,
>
> Missy

Dear Santa Claus:

How come David Letterman only does "stupid dog tricks"?

What has he got against cats?

> Your fan,
>
> Amy

Dear Santa:

The little girl who lives here, too, told you that she wants a dog. But you know what would be better? A goldfish or parakeet. They're much easier to take care of and nobody has to walk them in the morning. That's what I think she really would like.

Tiger

Dear Santa:

Is there a birth control pill for cats?

I don't want to be neutered.

Love,

Hazel

Dear Santa:

Do you have cat roller blades?

The dog chases me all the time.

Your pal,

Titus

Dear Santa:

I've been a good cat all year but please come quick.

I can't stay good much longer.

                              Love,

                              George

Dear Santa Claus:

I am an old cat.

All I want for Xmas is an autographed picture of Morris the Cat.

The kittens don't even remember Morris.

                              Vicky

Dear Santa Claus:

**I wash myself every day but the kids in
this family never wash.**

Please leave soap.

> **Love,**
>
> **Cindy**

Dear Santa Claus:

Please get me a new vet for Xmas.

**The vet they take me to pokes me all the
time.**

> **Love,**
>
> **Elisa**

Dear Santa:

The food in this house is terrible.

Could you please get me for Christmas some of the stuff that French cats eat?

Khat

Dear Santa:

We need new carpeting, Santa. I thought it would be a nice home improvement if I decorated the carpeting with a little of my very attractive, personal spray, but it turns out the others in this household were a little upset about it. They took up the old carpeting and have just left the bare wood floor, which is very cold and hard on my little paws in the morning.

Love,

Cute-ee-pie

Dear Santa Claus:

I was going to send you a Christmas card but the dog ate it.

Tabby

Dear Santa:

**For Christmas I would like all the pizzas
that Beth and Jim (my masters) order to
be with double anchovies.**

Antonio

Dear Santa:

I would like to live with Oprah.

Thank you.

Cynthia

P.S. She already has a dog.

Dear Santa Claus:

Please don't be cheap.

I don't want another ball of string for Xmas.

Your friend,

Jessie

Dear Santa Claus:

Could you get a new family for me?

This family doesn't understand cats. They think I throw up in the closet on purpose.

> **Your friend,**
>
> **Dexter**

Dear Santa Claus:

This is the last letter I am writing to you.

I don't believe in Santa anymore.

I am not a kitten now. I am a cat.

> **Cindy**

Dear Santa:

Are there any dogs at the North Pole?

If the answer is no I would like to visit.

Your friend,

Admiral

Dear Santa:

Do you have any catnip?

I'm off the wagon—again.

Your friend,

Pinky

Dear Santa Claus:

I would like to sit on your lap in the department store.

I promise not to scratch or shed.

Love,

Alfonse

Dear Santa:

Do you have a book on what to name your cat?

There are five kittens in the house and they call all of us Tabby.

Thank you,

Tabby #3

Dear Santa Claus:

How come there isn't a TV show about cats—like *Lassie?*

Cats are smarter and prettier than dogs.

Your friend,

Aggie

Dear Santa:

Is there a Dr. Spock book for cats?

I would like such a book because I am expecting kittens.

Jezebel

Dear Santa:

I would love a ticket to the circus so I can see the tigers.

They're relatives of mine.

Your friend,

Stripes

Dear Santa:

Could you bring my person a bigger house? How about the White House? I'm a fat cat and I need more space.

Gatsby

Dear Santa Claus:

I want my own TV set.

They never let me watch *Wild Kingdom*.

Sherlock

Dear Santa Claus:

If you leave me a book for Xmas, please make it *The Cat In The Hat* by Dr. Seuss.

Thank you,

Rascal

Dear Santa:

**Please take me with you. I don't get a
chance to hunt or fish here in New York
City. (I don't even get to go outside!) Maybe
I could do some ice fishing at the North Pole
when things aren't to busy. I promise to be a
good worker when you need me to be.**

> **Your future elf cat,**
>
> **James**

Dear Santa:

I would like to visit the ASPCA.

That's where I was born.

> **Your fan,**
>
> **Paws**

Dear Santa:

I like your beard.

I have whiskers too!

                                    Steve

Dear Santa:

Could you please leave a kitten?

I'm tired of being the baby of the family.

Love,

Trixie

Dear Santa Claus:

I would like you to take the dog to the North Pole and not bring him back until next Christmas.

Jerome

Dear Santa:

What did you do before you were Santa Clause?

Were you ever a vet? You look like my vet except that you are fatter and my vet never wears a red suit.

Calvin

Dear Santa Claus:

All I want for Christmas is a picture of you riding on your Christmas sled. I already have a picture of you coming down the chimney.

**Love,
Andy**

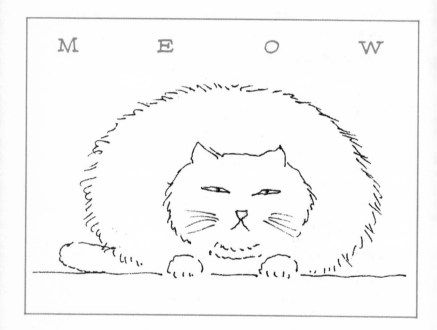

Dear Santa:

Does Weight Watchers have anything for cats?

I'm so fat I even meow in slow motion.

Denise

Dear Santa Claus:

I would like to ride with you in your sled on Christmas eve.

I promise not to scratch the upholstery.

Love,

Pumpkin

Dear Santa:

Could I have ear plugs for Xmas?

The new baby is keeping me up all night.

Love,

Helen

Dear Santa:

I would like two tickets to the show *Cats* for Christmas.

Me and my best friend, Tabby, want to have a night on the town.

> Thank you,
>
> Eliot

Dear Santa Claus:

This Xmas please leave a short-haired kitten and take back the long-haired kitten.

I think I'm allergic to long-haired cats.

> Your friend,
>
> Tyrone

Dear Santa Claus:

I need a place to sleep.

The lady got married again and the new guy doesn't want me in the bed.

Love,

Sam

Dear Santa:

I would like a picture of Mickey Mouse that I can pin up in my room.

Your friend,

Minnie

Dear Santa:

I need a book on how to deal with a neurotic human.

Thank you,

Freud

Dear Santa Claus:

I would like to meet a nice tom cat from a good neighborhood.

All the toms around here are lowlifes.

Your friend,

Dennis

Dear Santa Claus:

I would like a cat dictionary.

There must be other things I can say besides "meow."

Sincerely,

Malcolm

Dear Santa Claus:

I would like to be the mascot for the New York Yankees.

I think they could use me for good luck.

Your friend,

B. B.

Dear Santa Claus:

I would like to have Madonna's address.

I want to write her. Maybe she would like a cat.

Life around here is real dull.

Your fan,

Lionel

Dear Santa Claus:

Please get the family a kitten.

I am tired of being cute all the time.

Your friend,

Toonces

Dear Santa:

I know you have reindeer but do you have a cat?

I would like to be Santa's cat.

Love,

Cuddles

P.S. I don't mind cold weather.

Dear Santa:

I would like a cat pinup calendar. The cats around here are real dogs.

Love,

Fang

Dear Santa:

Please leave me a Christmas dinner prepared by The Frugal Gourmet.

I am sick of cat chow.

Your pal,

Amos

Dear Santa:

I need a book on how to train a dog.

This mutt is driving me crazy.

Your friend,

Tootles

Dear Santa:

**Please put under my Christmas tree
another Garfield book.**

My master won't return mine.

Love,

Simon

Dear Santa:

I know there's a Santa Claus for cats.

**The half-wit canine next door thinks
there's also a Santa for him.**

Tell me it's not true.

                              Ginny

Dear Santa Claus:

**Please leave them a book about cat sounds
so they will know what I want when I
meow.**

                    Thank you.

                    Victoria

Dear Santa:

I am a black cat so everybody thinks I bring bad luck.

Do you have a good luck charm I could wear around my neck.

Thank you.

Love,

Ebony

Dear Santa:

These people expect me to do tricks all the time.

I think you better get them a dog.

Love,

Penn

Dear Santa:

I would like another cat to play with.

The Siamese you left last year keeps me up all night talking.

Your friend,

Lucy

Dear Santa Claus:

Please get me a big cat litter box.

They still think I'm a kitten.

Love,

Jacob

P.S. I wouldn't mind a litter box cover for a little privacy, either.

Dear Santa:

Please don't leave any more cat training or cat trick books. They don't understand these don't work.

Your friend,

Homer

Dear Santa Claus:

Do you have cat mittens you could give me for Xmas?

They are blaming me for scratching everything.

Love,

Carson

Dear Santa:

I would like my own comic strip.

I'm as cute as Felix.

> Your friend,
>
> Narcissus

Dear Santa:

Please leave a mouse trap. I'm thinking of laying off the rodents and becoming a vegetarian.

> Thank you,
>
> Tom

Dear Santa Claus:

I need more privacy. The family has privacy. The dog has his own house. Even the canary has her own space.

My litter box is right out in the open.

Morgan

Dear Santa:

I left one of my cat treats for you under the Christmas tree.

If you don't want to eat it, you can give it to a cat at the North Pole.

Love,

Katrinka

Dear Santa:

I desperately need a new computer so I can talk to other cats on the Internet.

OK, it's my fault the old one doesn't work. I honestly thought the mouse was a toy so I kind of batted it around. By the time I realized the fish was a screen saver the moniter was pretty scratched. And if I'm not supposed to nap on the thing why did they make it so toasty warm? It's like a magnet for furballs.

I promise to take better care of my new machine.

Love,

Einstein Two

Dear Santa:

I would like to go on the next space shuttle trip.

I want to be the first cat on the moon.

> **Your friend,**
>
> **Serine**

Dear Santa:

Please leave a cat cookbook for the lady.

Her food isn't fit for a dog.

> **Your cat,**
>
> **Jack Sprat**

Dear Santa Claus:

Here is what I would like for Xmas:

> **1. A mouse**
>
> **2. A goldfish**
>
> **3. A bird**
>
> **4. A new chair for the living room.**

Thank you,

Rambo

Dear Santa Claus:

Please don't leave anything for the dog.

The dog never shares anything with me.

Your friend,

Damon

Dear Santa Claus:

Please wake me up when you come to our house.

The cat down the block says you don't really exist.

Love,

Petunia

Dear Santa:

Please leave under the Xmas tree a gift box wrapped in ribbon.

The box can be empty.

All I want is the ribbon.

Love,

Lulabelle

Dear Santa:

Please leave me some egg nog for Xmas.

Milk is boring.

> Love,
>
> Skipper

Dear Santa Claus:

I hope you leave me something for Xmas.

I have been a good cat all year.

> Love,
>
> Sly

P.S. They left you milk and cookies but I drank the milk.

Dear Santa Claus:

I would like a toy mouse for Xmas so I can practice. (The real ones get away and then they point at me and laugh.)

Your pal,

Tabitha

Dear Santa:

I know us cats are supposed to have nine lives but I think I'll need more than that with the new baby they just got around here.

Your friend,

Auggie

Dear Santa Claus:

Could you leave a fake cat tail for the baby?

Then maybe she won't pull mine all the time.

Love,

Peaches

Dear Santa:

There's a little bird that sits in the tree all day outside my window.

That's what I want for Xmas.

Love,

Cinders

Dear Santa Claus:

Do you have a machine that makes a purring noise?

I'm getting sick and tired of purring all the time just to make them happy.

Yours,

Cecil

Dear Santa Claus:

Why do *dogs* do so many stupid tricks?

**Could you teach me one trick I could do
so they will leave me alone?**

Your friend,

Houdini

Dear Santa Claus:

For Christmas, all I want is a vet that makes house calls. I'm tired of making the trip in that box.

> **Your friend.**
>
> **Phineas**

Dear Santa:

Please find me a Tom before they fix me. Quick!

> **Your pal,**
>
> **Suzette**

Dear Santa:

I hate to be finicky but this year, could you leave something in my bowl besides tuna?

Love,

Orca

Dear Santa:

We need new drapes in the living room before *she* sees what I did to the old ones.

Your friend,

Polly

Dear Santa:

Could you please leave the faucet on for me? I like that water in the sink better than the water in the bowl.

Squeaky

Dear Santa:

Could you please send me the names of all the good cats in the neighborhood?

I don't want to hang out with bad cats any more.

Ricky

Dear Santa Claus:

I have been a good cat all year if you don't count the drapes, the sofa, and the slippers.

Your friend,

Bott